Life is... Ruff

by Chris Howard

SNIFF
SNIFF

Illustrated by Stephanie Arnal

My name is Cody, and I am happy to say I turned fifteen-years-old today. All my friends came over to play and celebrate my special day. We had doggie ice cream, and even doggie cake. Good times for all, for goodness' sake. Fifteen years is a good long life, I'm told, But believe it or not, I still don't feel old!

My rescue was the best when I was a pup,

until I grew all the way up. Yup!

My life has been so fun, and so great.

I do believe, it was all just fate.

The day I saw Chris from behind those cold bars,

I knew, there would be no more dodging cars.

I would be safe and cared for, it would be so neat,

because before I met him, I lived on the street.

In a box with no heat

is where I would sleep.

It was scary and cold, with nothing to eat,

and all I wanted was a couple of treats.

I was lonely there, all by myself.

Then I became worried about my health.

Something was wrong with my sense of smell.

But what was the cause? I couldn't quite tell.

My nose was very runny,

and there was no food in my tummy.

I really just felt crumby

I always had a strong will to live,

and a lot of love I wanted to give.

Although my life seemed grim

I believed that I would soon meet him.

I never gave up, because of the size of my heart.

If you met me, you would know that from the start.

As the sniffles got worse, and the sun grew dim,

I made a wish that someday, I'd find him!

He would take me hiking, and play all day.

He would feed me yummy food, and

make my cold go away!

Then I would grow to be healthy, and strong.

The lonely days on the street, would soon be all gone!

As these visions of my new friend ran through my mind,

I imagined he would never leave me behind.

As the sun went down, and the night grew dark,

I imagined us playing fetch at the park. When he lifts up

the stick, I'll let out a bark.

As he threw it far, he would watch me run.

And I'd wag my tail from all the fun.

As my eyes grew heavy, I heard my stomach growl.

When the moon came out, I let out a lonely howl

"Ow oww owwwwwwwwwww!"

It's back to the box, and it feels so hollow,

with a blanket inside, that I had to borrow!

I did not know this would be my last day.

Just one more night, and I'm off and I'm on my way!

It was time for me to get some rest.

So I pushed the blanket around and made a nest.

Before very long, I started to dream

about someday being part of a team.

Together, we would laugh and play.

With him, I'd happily stay.

I dreamed of the pair we'd be,

I'd love him, and he'd love me.

This dream I had seemed so real.

If given the chance, his heart, I would steal!

Together forever! We will make a deal!

In the morning, I woke to the sound of a truck.

As I climbed out of my box, I remembered to duck!

Otherwise I would probably get stuck.

There a friendly man stood.

He kept the rain off his head with a hood.

His uniform was all buttoned up.

He saw me, and came over to pick me right up!

He had his coffee in one hand, in the other his net.

And he said," Someone will take you home I bet!"

He gave me some kibble,

so I took a small nibble. I was a bit nervous, just a little.

We drove to a shelter outside of the city

The friendly man in uniform was sure he could help me!

He gave me some medicine, and what do you know?

I felt better from my ears to my nose.

He gave me some water from the hose,

then he plopped me in a cage, and I heard the door close.

Attached to my cage was a small letter that read,

"Stray #1507, soon to be dead!"

I couldn't believe what that cage card said.

The visions of him were still stuck in my head!

I was hungry, and it was time to be fed,

and no comfort could be found without a blanket or bed.

In the cage there was nothing to do.

There was not even a pillow to chew.

I was surrounded by nothing but metal

that made me feel blue and very unsettled.

As the days went by,

I hoped and wished and tried not to cry.

The kennel blues was beginning to linger,

when one day a boy came in, and he let me lick his finger.

I saw in his eyes that he was the one.

We would soon be having fun.

He was just like the dream, the one I had in that box!

Only now he was here, and this cage had locks!!

I had to do something, so he wouldn't walk away.

Now was my chance to get him to stay!

Although I was sick, I jumped to my feet.

I pawed at the bars for one more peek.

If he opens the cage, I'll kiss his cheek.

Otherwise I could be dead in a week!

I knew if he saw me, he would fall in love.

I sensed his visit was a gift from above.

He tried to ignore me, as I made a big fuss.

Then he finally turned to say,"What's all the ruckus?"

I continued my happy dance, and was cute as could be.

It was my puppy dog eyes; it had to be!

He laughed and came over to the cage.

Was this the beginning of my new life? Can I turn the page?

He then said to me, "what a sweet little pup.

Do you want me to pick you up?"

He spoke to me and I couldn't ignore;

I could hardly keep my paws on the cage floor.

Then I jumped right on that metal cage door.

I wiggled all over, right down to my core!

Chin down, tail up, as I postured over.

I will be his good luck charm, like a four-leaf clover!

When I saw his hand reach for that cage latch,

I said a quick prayer, and I hoped he could catch.

As soon as the door opened, I leapt to his chest.

He put his arms around me. "Ahhhhhhh, this was the best!"

Then I wrapped my head around the back of his neck;

I heard him chuckle and say, "What the heck?"

He held me snugly in that old room.

I knew that soon our friendship would bloom.

As I rested my head on his shoulder,

I felt a weight lift, like the size of a boulder!

He said "You are OK now, baby pup!"

And I noticed his eyes began to fill up.

They started to glisten from a tiny tear.

Then he spoke softly in my right ear.

He said, "You are a good girl, I can surely see!"

I knew from that very moment, I would have to be!

Then I noticed a tiny tear fall from his face.

It was then, I could see, I would get out of this place!

It was a sign! That clue!

All along I knew.

My dreams came true

and it was a good thing, too.

I was on borrowed time

but now I would be fine.

Good times for us, were certainly near.

I could tell by that tiny first tear,

that finally I had nothing to fear.

Ow owww, I was getting out of here!

Until now it's been a bit ruff

Although a pup, I'm still pretty tough!

I made it past that test,

and soon I could forget about the rest

This was the beginning of something sweet.

I tingled all over, down to all four puppy feet!

I must have touched him, with my wet nose,

and warm heart.

From that day forward, we would never be apart!

He collected himself, and he carried me out the door.

He said, "I'll call you Cody girl," and then hugged me

some more.

Since the day he saved me, we have been best friends.

He promised he would ALWAYS be there to the end!

He took me everywhere he went.

With me, his time was always spent.

We played in fields of flowers, and romped through

the woods, too!

We took walks in the morning, when the sky was blue.

As time goes on, our bond grew stronger.

I think that is why my life is longer.

He gave me a happy home and love without fear.

And today we celebrate my fifteenth year.

The love we shared was so sweet and pure.

I even liked the sound, when he snored!

He also taught me to be secure!

Chris, always, tried to spoil me.

There was something about him, you can't always see.

He is hoof-hearted! It is a bit oversized!

I said thank you, again, for his dark eyes.

They always sparkled, and gleamed!

Everything in my life, turned out like I'd dreamed!

I could tell he was the one, the one I dreamed for.

I felt all the love he had in store.

I could feel his heartbeat, right through my chest.

As far as friends go, he was the best.

If it is up to me, he passed my test!

Like two hearts together, beating in sync.

It was love at first sight, I like to think!

Now I have to go and play!

Did I mention it's my birthday today?

So I think for my wish, it will have to be,

that I can help him, as much, as he helped me!

Thanks for listening to my story, about Chris and me!

I am getting old now, so I got to go pee!

Just remember in your local shelter,

there are puppies like me.

Pups need homes all over this country!

Maybe, just maybe, you will see,

there is one there dreaming of you,

and maybe, just maybe, holding your heart's key!

Then you can give her a happy life too!

Just remember when walking her, she picked you!

For more pictures of Codygirl visit

www.TheAnimalHaus-MA.com or visit Cody's Fan page

on facebookTheAnimalHaus

Also Please Support Your Local Shelters.

Visit LowellHumaneSociety.org for a list of pets that

need homes. Spread the word.